MW00974951

Bill Gates
Software Genius of Microsoft

INTERNET BIOGRAPHIES

INTERNET BIOGRAPHIES

Bill Gates
Software Genius of Microsoft

by Craig Peters

Enslow Publishers, Inc.

40 Industrial Road   PO Box 38
Box 398   Aldershot
Berkeley Heights, NJ 07922   Hants GU12 6BP
USA   UK

http://www.enslow.com

PRODUCED BY:
Chestnut Productions
Russell, Massachusetts

Editor and Picture Researcher: *Mary E. Hull*
Design and Production: *Lisa Hochstein*

Copyright © 2003 by Enslow Publishers, Inc.

All rights reserved

No part of this book may be reproduced by any means without the written permission of the publisher.

Library of Congress Cataloging-in-Publication Data

Peters, Craig, 1958-
   Bill Gates : software genius of Microsoft / by Craig Peters.
      p. cm. — (Internet biographies)
Summary: Explores the life and career of the software developer and computer entrepreneur, discussing his early efforts in co-founding Microsoft, current successes and problems of the company, and his philanthropy.
Includes bibliographical references and index.
   ISBN 0-7660-1969-1
   1. Gates, Bill, 1955- —Juvenile literature. 2. Businessmen—United States—Biography—Juvenile literature. 3. Computer software industry—United States—History—Juvenile literature. 4. Microsoft Corporation—History—Juvenile literature. [1. Gates, Bill, 1955-
2. Businesspeople. 3. Computer software industry. 4. Microsoft Corporation—History.] I. Title. II. Series.
HD9696.63.U62 G3748 2003
338.7'610053'092—dc21   2002153176

Printed in the United States of America

10 9 8 7 6 5 4 3 2 1

To Our Readers:
We have done our best to make sure all Internet addresses in this book were active and appropriate when we went to press. However, the author and the publisher have no control over and assume no liability for the material available on those Internet sites or on other Web sites they may link to. Any comments or suggestions can be sent by e-mail to comments@enslow.com or to the address on the back cover.

Illustration Credits: Associated Press/Wide World Photos, pp. 2, 6, 9, 21, 22, 26, 30, 35, 36, 38; Corbis, pp. 10, 24, 26.

Cover Illustration: Associated Press/Wide World Photos

Opposite Title Page: Microsoft chairman Bill Gates is also the company's chief software architect. He unveiled the Windows XP operating system in 2001. Windows XP helped businesses to take advantage of the digital world.

CONTENTS

Bill Gates speaks about the need for vaccinating children in poor countries. Gates has used his enormous wealth to fund programs that improve global health.

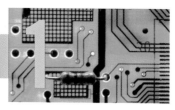

Giving Back

On September 18, 1997, billionaire businessman Ted Turner made headlines around the world. Turner, who created the Cable News Network (CNN), said he would contribute $1 billion to the United Nations. It was a huge amount of money.

"What good is wealth sitting in the bank?" Turner had asked during a speech five months earlier. "It's a pretty pathetic thing to do with your money."[1] Many people thought the comment was a challenge to other very wealthy businessmen, especially Bill Gates, the co-founder of Microsoft.

Gates probably heard about Turner's challenge. At the time, Gates was the second richest man in the world, behind only Sultan Hassanal Bolkiah of Brunei, a small country in south Asia. Gates's personal fortune was about $40 billion.[2]

Yet Gates was no stranger to charitable giving. In 1994, years before Ted Turner's challenge, he had established the William H. Gates Foundation. The

Foundation gave away many millions of dollars.[3] In 1996, Gates donated $135 million to cancer research and a children's hospital. In 1997, he donated $200 million to put computers in libraries that could not afford them.[4] Early in 1997, Gates created the Bill and Melinda Gates Foundation, which gave away money to groups that improved people's health and education.

However, in the years following Turner's speech, Gates's donations to charity increased dramatically.

In September, 1999, the Bill and Melinda Gates Foundation pledged $1 billion over twenty years to the United Negro College Fund. Three months later, the foundation donated $750 million over five years to The Vaccine Fund, to help prevent disease in seventy-four countries.[5] In 2000, $685.5 million, nearly half of the foundation's giving, went to improve people's health around the world.

THE RICHEST PERSON IN THE WORLD

Bill Gates has been ranked by *Forbes*, a leading business magazine, as the richest person in the world for many years in a row. Here is a chart of Gates's wealth:

1995	$12.9 billion
1996	$18.5 billion
1997	$36.4 billion
1998	$51 billion
1999	$90 billion
2000	$60 billion
2001	$58.7 billion

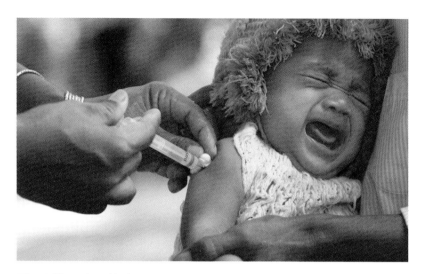

The Bill and Melinda Gates Foundation has donated millions to The Vaccine Fund, which protects children from disease.

"People are a little surprised that my focus in philanthropy—over 60 percent of what the foundation's doing—relates to world health," Gates said in 2001. "It doesn't relate to computers and software. We do some of that . . . but I've decided the thing that counts the most is world health."[6]

When Gates gives away money to help world health, that means a lot to the world. The Bill and Melinda Gates Foundation is the largest charitable organization on the planet. As *The New York Times* reported in April 2000, "Even the greatest philanthropists of the past did not give away as much in real dollars over their entire lifetimes as Gates has at the age of forty-four."[7]

Not bad for a guy who did not finish college.

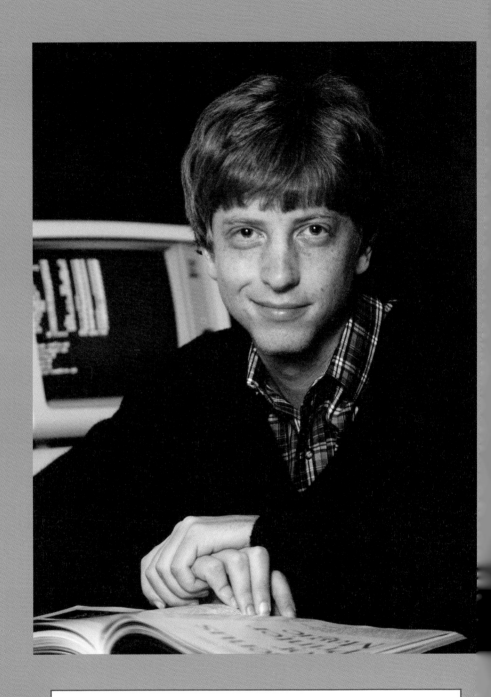

Bill Gates has always been fascinated by computers. In high school he and his friends formed a programmers' club. They spent hours sharing the school's one computer, learning how it worked.

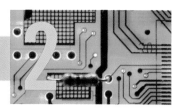

Deep Roots
in Seattle

Wiilliam Henry Gates III was born to Bill and Mary Gates on October 28, 1955, in Seattle, Washington. Bill was the middle of three children and the only boy. His sister Kristi was one year older, and his sister Libby was nine years younger.

"My dad was a lawyer and my mom was very involved in business," Gates recalled in 1993. "They shared what they were doing out in the world with my older sister and I as we were growing up. So we always had a sense of, 'Okay, this is the Governor coming to dinner, or here is this political campaign, let's get involved in this.'"[1]

Bill's nickname growing up was "Trey," a reference to him being the third William H. Gates in the family. The nickname "Trey" probably came from card playing. In cards, "trey" is a nickname for a three, just like "deuce" is a nickname for a two. Bill's grandfather was vice-president of a bank, and his great-grandfather was the founder of Seattle's National City Bank.

Gates attended public elementary school.He especially liked math and science. He was a good student, but he didn't always get along with his parents. According to *Time* magazine, Gates and his mother were "at war" during this time in his life.[2]

When he was in the sixth grade, for example, his mother, Mary, would call him up to dinner from his basement bedroom and he wouldn't always respond.

"What are you doing?" she once demanded.

"I'm thinking," he shouted back.

"You're thinking?"

"Yes, Mom, I'm thinking," he said fiercely. "Have you ever tried thinking?"[3]

Years later, the *Washington Post* described Gates as a very smart child who spent a lot of time alone. The newspaper article described the rocking motion that takes place when Gates is thinking seriously. "He tucks his elbows into his thighs and brings his chin almost to his kneecaps. When he's thinking hard, he rocks faster."[4] To this day, Gates often displays this rocking motion during interviews and in meetings.

Not quite sure how to deal with Bill, Mary sent her son to a psychologist, "a really cool guy," Gates recalled. "He gave me books to read after each session." After a year, the doctor reached his conclusion. "You're going to lose," he told Mary. "You had better just adjust to it, because there's no use trying to beat him."[5]

Part of Mary's adjustment included sending her 12-year-old son to Lakeside, a private school in the

Seattle area. At Lakeside, Gates met Paul Allen, who became his best friend and, later, his business partner. Lakeside also introduced Gates to computers.

"At first I really didn't like the environment [at school]," Gates recalled in a 1993 interview. "I did eventually find some friends there, some of whom had the same sort of interests, like reading business magazines and *Fortune*. We were always creating funny company names and having people send us

BILL GATES'S FIRST COMPUTER EXPERIENCE

At the Lakeside School, Bill Gates worked on an ASR-33 teletype computer terminal. It was a common computer terminal in the 1970s. "ASR" stood for "Automatic Send Receive." The terminal, manufactured by the Teletype Corporation, looked like a heavy-duty typewriter. The keys took a lot of effort to press.

The ASR-33 was not a computer, but it did provide access to a computer. It was more like a very bulky keyboard, connected through the phone to a computer miles away. Information was fed into the ASR-33 on long spools of paper punched with tiny holes. The terminal then sent the information to a main computer through the telephone. The cost of an ASR-33 terminal in the early 1970s was $1,400. That's about the same as a complete computer today. But the ASR-33 only connected to a computer, it wasn't a computer all by itself. The ASR-33 teletype printed at a speed of about ten letters per second. Today, many home computer printers can print at a speed of about 200 letters per second.

Bill Gates, left, and Paul Allen, the co-founders of Microsoft, met in high school. They discovered they both liked to write programs and fix computer glitches.

their product literature. Trying to think about how business worked. And in particular, looking at computer companies and what was going on with them."[6]

Gates, Allen, and several others began spending time together working on the school computer. They learned as much as possible about computers and how to write computer programs. Their knowledge of computers got them a job with the Computer Center Corporation. Gates and his friends would find bugs, or errors, in the computer system, and Computer Center Corporation gave them all the time they wanted to spend on the computer.

The Computer Center Corporation went out of business in 1970, but Gates and his buddies, who called themselves the Lakeside Programmers Group, were just getting started. Gates and Paul Allen created a computer program called Traf-O-Data to measure traffic on city streets. Traf-O-Data kept track of how many cars used a road. It then used that information to create reports for the state's road department. The road department could decide how much money to set aside for repairs, or where to place traffic lights.[7]

During their junior year at Lakeside, Gates and Allen were asked by the school to create a program for scheduling classes. A year later, they got jobs at TRW, a company that worked with the U.S. military. The jobs were similar to what they did for the Computer Center Corporation. Instead of just finding bugs in the system, though, they also had to fix them.

In the fall of 1973 Gates entered Harvard University. "I knew that if I wanted to be a lawyer or a mathematician, Harvard had good courses for these things," Gates said.

> Once I got there, I thought economics was pretty interesting. And I felt that I understood computers well enough that I really didn't need to hang out with a computer crowd there, because they weren't as interesting. I did end up taking a few computer courses. But most of what I did was not related to computers.[8]

Gates and Allen continued to be close friends. They paid close attention to news about the computer field. In December 1974, their lives changed. They saw the future on the cover of a seventy-five cent magazine.

In 1975, Bill Gates teamed up with his friend Paul Allen to write software for the Altair 8800, a build-it-yourself kit computer made by the MITS company.

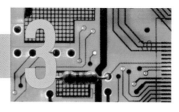

CHAPTER

A Computer in Every Home

Bill Gates and Paul Allen read the January 1975 issue of *Popular Electronics* with special interest. "Project Breakthrough!" the headline on the cover screamed in bold red type. "World's First Mini-computer Kit to Rival Commercial Models—Altair 8800—Save Over $1,000." Inside the magazine, the story seemed too good to be true. "The era of the computer in every home—a favorite topic among science-fiction writers—has arrived!"[1] Gates and Allen understood that something very important was happening.

"It was kind of, in a way, good news and bad news," Gates recalled years later. "Here was someone making this computer around this chip in exactly the way that Paul had talked to me, and we'd thought about what kind of software could be done for it, and it was happening without us."[2]

Micro Instrumentation and Telemetry Systems (MITS) was the maker of the Altair 8800. Shortly after they saw the magazine, Gates and Allen contacted MITS, saying that they had a version of the BASIC computer language that would run on the Altair 8800. BASIC, which stands for Beginner's All-purpose Symbolic Instruction Code, was a simple computer language in common use at the time. MITS was interested, but they did not realize that Gates and Allen had only enthusiasm to work with. They did not even have an Altair 8800.

That didn't stop them. Using information about the Altair and his own smarts, Gates wrote most of the code (the written instructions that would be fed into the computer) for the BASIC program. The program did a variety of simple math calculations. Allen flew to New Mexico to show the program to MITS. It was the first time that Allen had seen an Altair 8800 outside the pages of *Popular Electronics.*

Paul Allen ran the program for Ed Roberts, the head of MITS. It worked!

MITS wanted to use the software that Gates and Allen had written. They worked out a contract to provide software programming services. Paul Allen moved to New Mexico and was hired by MITS as Director of Software Development. In the meantime, he kept working with Gates part-time.

In 1975, Gates and Allen named their new business "Micro-soft", a combination of the words "microcomputer" and "software." (The hyphen was later dropped from the name.) The company's first five clients went bankrupt, but Gates and Allen did not give up. Before long Micro-soft was developing versions of BASIC for major companies like General Electric and Citibank.

Gates dropped out of Harvard in his junior year to follow his friend out west. After eighteen months at MITS, Allen left the company to join Micro-soft full time. Micro-soft developed additional programming languages and even won its first lawsuit: a 1977 battle with MITS over the ownership rights to their version of BASIC.

By the end of 1978, Micro-soft sales exceeded $1 million. In 1979, the company dropped the hyphen, became Microsoft, and moved to the Seattle area.

WHAT IS AN OPERATING SYSTEM?

The operating system is the program on the computer that controls how the computer works. It understands that when you type "dog" on the keyboard, you mean to say "dog" and not "cat," "top," "big," or some other combination of three letters. The operating system lets a person talk to the computer and tell it what to do. It also lets different computer programs talk to each other.

When IBM asked Microsoft for an operating system for its personal computer, it was like the head of a country asking someone, "What language should my people speak?" It meant that Microsoft could decide how people would work with computers.

Late in 1980, IBM came to Microsoft and asked Gates to provide an operating system, the software that allows a computer to operate, for the company's first personal computer. It was a very big break. For the first time, a major company was planning to sell personal computers to the public. Microsoft purchased an operating system called 86-QDOS from a company called Seattle Computer for $50,000,

THE EXPLOSION OF PC SALES

When IBM introduced the personal computer (PC) in the fall of 1981, they hoped it would be a success. They had no idea how successful it would become. In the final months of 1981, IBM sold 35,000 machines—five times the expected sales.

Personal computer sales continued to skyrocket throughout the 1980s. According to *PC Magazine*, the total annual PC sales in the United States in 1981 amounted to 671,537 units. By 1983 that number had risen to 1.3 million computers. In 1986 there were nearly 4.4 million units sold in the United States. In 1989 the number of computers sold was just over 9 million.

All of these computers ran on the MS-DOS operating system, which meant a lot of licensing fees for Microsoft. Beyond the MS-DOS operating software, however, the machines required additional software programs so users could do word processing, keep financial records, and play games. Microsoft created many of these kinds of programs, too. As more people bought computers and wanted to do more things with them, Microsoft made lots more money.

This is the first IBM personal computer, released in 1981. It was outfitted with a monitor, printer, and Microsoft's MS-DOS software. Microsoft earned a royalty on every copy of the software.

changed the name of the program to MS-DOS, and licensed it to IBM. Each time a computer with MS-DOS software was sold, Microsoft earned money from the software.

The IBM personal computer was a huge success, and Microsoft made a great deal of money. By the end of 1982, the company had doubled in size, earning $34 million and putting 200 people to work.

Just seven years after Gates and Allen formed Microsoft, *Time* magazine, which usually chooses a "Man of the Year" at the end of each year, named the personal computer "Machine of the Year." Gates's vision of a computer on every desktop was well on its way to becoming true. Microsoft was positioned at the very center of the computer revolution.

Microsoft's operating system uses a graphic interface, which lets computer users click on images on the screen to tell the computer what to do. A mouse, shown at bottom right, made it easy for users to click on symbols.

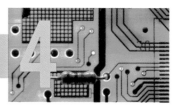

Billionaires and Browser Wars

The 1980s were a time of incredible growth and innovation for Bill Gates and Microsoft. In 1983, the company introduced its Microsoft Word word processing program. It also announced that it would soon be introducing a graphic interface for PCs known as Windows 1.0. With a graphic interface, the computer user clicks on pictures and symbols to ask the computer to perform functions instead of having to type specific commands into the system. For example, clicking on a small picture of a printer to print a document was much easier than having to type "PRINT [/B:(buffersize)] [/D:(device)] [/M:(maxtick)] [/Q:(value)] [/S:(timeslice)] [/U:(busytick)] [/C] [/P] [/T] [d:] [path] [filename]."

In the early 1980s, the biggest competitor to the IBM personal computer was the Apple computer. Apple computers were first introduced in 1976, and by 1983 Apple had sold 1 million computers. In 1984, Apple Computer released the Macintosh computer, which used a graphic interface that was far more user-friendly than anything that had been released up to that time. Microsoft soon began releasing various programs for the Macintosh.

Windows 1.0 was finally released in September 1985. It was widely criticized as a crude imitation of the Macintosh operating system. Windows 2.0 followed in 1987, but it wasn't very popular either.

Then came Windows 3.0 in 1990. It was also criticized for being too similar to Apple's Macintosh interface. Still, it was a big improvement over earlier versions of Windows. The software sold more than 10 million copies. Two years later, Windows 3.1 sold 3 million copies in its first two months on sale.

Meanwhile, on March 13, 1986, Microsoft became a public company, which meant that shares of ownership in the company could be bought and sold on the stock market. The price of one share of Microsoft stock that day was $21. Gates owned 11,142,000 shares of stock. That meant he was worth about $234 million.[1] A year later, Microsoft stock reached $90 per share. Gates became a billionaire at the age of thirty-one.[2]

In the first half of the 1990s Microsoft enjoyed huge successes. In 1990, the company's sales were more than $1 billion for the first time. Windows 95 software was released in 1995. It sold 7 million copies in the first six weeks.

Gates enjoyed personal success during this time, too. In 1993, he was awarded the National Medal of

Technology by President Bush. On January 1, 1994, he married Melinda French in Hawaii. Sadly, there was tragedy, too: Gates's mother, Mary, died of breast cancer later that year.

In 1995, Gates's first book, *The Road Ahead,* was published. The book, dedicated to his parents, became a best-seller. In the book's foreword, Gates wrote "the revolution in communications is just

HOW MUCH IS A BILLION DOLLARS?

In 1986, Bill Gates became a billionaire at the age of thirty-one. It's hard to imagine a billion dollars. Try thinking of it like this: If you earned $1,000 a day, it would take you 2,740 years to earn a billion dollars. Here are a few more ways to understand how much $1 billion is:

- With $1 billion, you could buy a stack of compact discs 421 miles high (assuming each CD costs $15, and the CDs are still in their cases). If each of these discs contained forty-five minutes of music, and you started listening to them in 2003, you wouldn't finish listening to all the music until the year 7710.

- If you had a billion dollars in one dollar bills, and laid the dollars end to end, the line of dollars would stretch on for 943,696 miles. That's long enough to circle the earth almost four times.

- If you had a billion dollars in one dollar bills, sat down to count them all, and counted one each second, it would take you more than thirty years to finish counting!

Bill Gates sits on stage during the video portion of the Windows 95 software launch. Windows 95 debuted in 1995 and sold 7 million copies in the first six weeks.

beginning . . . . During the next few years, major decisions will have to be made by governments, companies, and individuals."[3]

One of the major decisions Gates might have been writing about was the choice of browser, the software used to see pages on the World Wide Web.

In 1995 and 1996, Netscape Navigator was the most popular browser. Almost three out of four computer users were Netscape users.[4] When Windows 95 came out, though, Microsoft's Internet Explorer browser was the default browser for computers with the Windows 95 operating system. This meant that unless users changed the browser preferences on their computers, they would end up using Internet Explorer. Microsoft software was running on 80 percent of the personal computers in the United States in 1997.[5] Netscape was losing users to Internet Explorer.

Controversy grew as Microsoft began preparing Windows 98, its next software upgrade. Netscape

INCREDIBLE GROWTH

The Microsoft story is one of amazing growth. The number of people employed by the corporation grew very quickly. So did the company's revenue, which is the amount of money the public spent on Microsoft products. Here is a look at the numbers since the company went public in 1986.

YEAR	EMPLOYEES	REVENUE
1986	1,153	$197.5 million
1987	1,816	$345.9 million
1988	2,793	$590.8 million
1989	4,037	$804.5 million
1990	5,635	$ 1.18 billion
1991	8,226	$ 1.85 billion
1992	11,542	$ 2.78 billion
1993	14,430	$ 3.79 billion
1994	15,017	$ 4.71 billion
1995	17,801	$ 6.08 billion
1996	20,561	$ 9.05 billion
1997	22,232	$ 11.94 billion
1998	27,055	$ 15.26 billion
1999	31,575	$ 19.75 billion
2000	39,170	$ 22.96 billion
2001	48,958	$ 25.30 billion

claimed that Microsoft was acting like a monopoly. In a monopoly, only one company has control over a product or service, and there is no competition in the marketplace. The company with the monopoly can raise its prices to customers who have nowhere else to go for the product. That is bad news for customers. A monopoly is illegal in the United States. The United States government got involved in the dispute between Netscape and Microsoft. It suggested that Microsoft include a copy of Netscape Navigator with every copy of Windows 98.

"It's indefensible that the government would try to force Microsoft and computer makers to give Netscape a free ride on every copy of our Windows operating system," said Mark Murray, a Microsoft spokesman. "Netscape clearly has a myriad of ways to distribute its product to customers. We don't think there's any basis in law to make such an unreasonable demand."[6]

The way the public used computers seemed to show Murray was right. The number of computer users using Internet Explorer grew from 2 percent in 1996 to 40 percent by October 1998. The number of people using Netscape dropped from 71 percent in 1996 to 60 percent in 1998. Fewer people were using Netscape, but it was still the most popular browser software.

Microsoft released the Windows 98 operating system in June 1998, one month after the Justice

Department filed an antitrust lawsuit against the company. The antitrust lawsuit meant that the government thought Microsoft was being unfair in the way it did business. The government thought Microsoft was acting like a monopoly.

The antitrust lawsuit was bad news for Microsoft, which was about to face its most difficult challenge of all.

The government accused Microsoft of crushing its competition. But Gates argued that Microsoft was actually encouraging innovation in the high-tech industry.

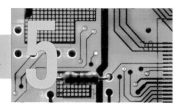

Trial by Fire

"Consumers and computer manufacturers should have the right to choose the software they want installed on their personal computers," said U.S. Attorney General Janet Reno on May 18, 1998. "We are acting to preserve competition and promote innovation in the computer software industry."[1]

Microsoft chairman and CEO Bill Gates responded by saying,

> Windows is popular because it offers consumers the best combination of price and performance. How ironic that in the United States—where freedom and innovation are core values—these regulators are trying to punish an American company that has worked hard and successfully to deliver on these values.[2]

With those words the battle lines were drawn. The Microsoft trial was watched closely around the world. There was no clear good guy and no clear bad guy. Everybody on both sides of the issue had a lot to say.

When the trial began on October 18, 1998, Microsoft president Steve Ballmer tried to keep Microsoft employees calm.

In an e-mail sent to Microsoft employees the night before the trial began, Ballmer wrote, ". . . we all must continue to stay focused on what we do best: serving the needs of our customers and creating products that really make a difference in people's lives."[3]

That, indeed, is what Gates and Microsoft tried to do. As the trial continued through June 1999, Microsoft worked toward the release of the latest version of Windows, Windows 2000. In March 1999 Gates released his second book, *Business @ the Speed of Thought,* which also became a best-seller.

Many experts predicted big trouble for Microsoft as a result of the trial. Many others weren't so sure.

THE MAN BEHIND MICROSOFT

When he's not working, Bill Gates enjoys spending time with his family. He and his wife Melinda have two children, Jennifer Katharine, born in 1996, and Rory John, born in 1999. Gates's hobbies include golf and the card game bridge. Gates also enjoys buying art and historical artifacts. He likes to read and arranges to meet with his favorite authors, sometimes flying them to Seattle.

Either way, the trial—not Microsoft's products—was becoming what people thought about when they thought of Bill Gates and Microsoft.

On November 5, 1999, the prediction of many experts came true. Microsoft was declared to be a monopoly. For Gates and his company, it was the worst thing that could happen.

Judge Thomas Penfield Jackson, U.S. District Judge for the District of Columbia, said, "Microsoft enjoys monopoly power in the relevant market."[4]

In response to Judge Jackson's decision, Gates said,

> The lawsuit is fundamentally about one question: Can a successful American company continue to improve its products for the benefit of consumers? That is precisely what Microsoft did by developing new versions of the Windows operating system with built-in support for the Internet.[5]

On January 13, 2000, with Microsoft's future looking very troubled, Bill Gates gave up day-to-day control of the company he co-founded. He handed the CEO position over to his close friend and former Harvard classmate, Steve Ballmer. Gates's decision made him "chief software architect," and he continued as chairman of the company.

After the decision was announced, some people said that Gates didn't want to be CEO during such troubled times. Gates dismissed the criticisms and called the timing of his decision a coincidence. "I'm returning to what I love most—focusing on technologies for the future,"[6] he said.

For the next several months, Microsoft and the United States government tried to work out a settlement. Microsoft hoped to avoid spending years in the courts. Microsoft also did not want the government to order the company to be split up into two companies. By early April 2000, though, it seemed that no settlement would be possible. On June 7, 2000, Judge Jackson ordered that Microsoft be broken up.

Judge Jackson's decision was appealed by Microsoft. A little more than one year later, on June 28, 2001, Jackson's ruling was overturned by a federal appeals court. The appeals court's ruling was a victory to Microsoft and a slap on the wrist to Judge Jackson.

The news was good for Gates, but there was still a lawsuit in the courts. Two months later, on August 29, a new judge was appointed to the case. Judge Coleen Kollar-Kotelly ordered both sides in the case to report back to her on any legal issues each side felt were still to be decided.

On September 6, 2001, the Justice Department said it no longer wanted to break up Microsoft into two companies. That was very good news for Gates, who did not have to worry about what might happen to his company. The lawsuit still needed to be settled, but now it looked like that could happen in a more friendly way. Gates did not have to live with the idea

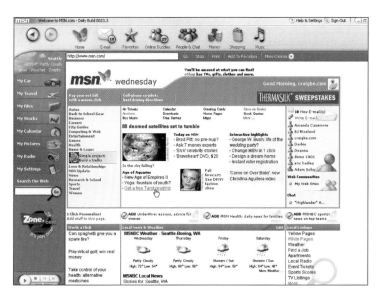

Microsoft is constantly coming up with new products. In 2000 it offered Microsoft Explorer, a new easy-to-use Web experience.

of Microsoft being replaced by two companies. He did not have to worry about which company he would work with, or what he would do with himself if Microsoft did not exist anymore.

By 2002, a settlement between Microsoft and the government seemed close. A major part of the settlement would be that Microsoft would contribute nearly $1 billion in computers, computer software, and computer training to schools nationwide.

After years of legal problems, Gates was once again looking forward to the future with a positive point of view.

Microsoft hoped to redesign gaming with the Xbox, a gaming console with high-tech speed, power, and graphics. The Xbox also has a "rumble" feature that makes the game controller vibrate in the player's hands. One of the new Xbox games was NFL Fever 2002.

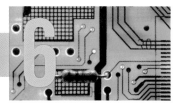

Epilogue

T here is no question that the story of Bill Gates is one of the most fascinating business stories of our time. His story is far from over.

In late 2001 Gates unveiled Microsoft's new XP operating system and the new Xbox gaming system. And yet to come is something that Gates says will send the world into a new computing revolution. It's called .Net and it is described by *eWeek* magazine as "a future platform that the software giant hopes will extend its Windows dynasty into the Internet era." The .Net initiative will allow computer users to access data from devices including PCs, handheld organizers, and cell phones. Gates calls it "a 'bet your company' strategy."[1] Will it mean more problems for Microsoft or will it carry the company to new heights of success?

Regardless of whether a new computer revolution happens or not, the world can certainly look forward to Gates's further charitable giving. The Microsoft

Bill Gates, right, poses with Intel chairman Andy Grove in 2001 for the twentieth anniversary of the personal computer. At either end are two of the oldest personal computers. At center are three of the newest laptops. Computer monitors, memory, and function have improved dramatically over the past twenty years.

co-founder has said that he plans to give away 98 percent of his wealth over time. That money is likely to go to various organizations that work to improve health and education worldwide.

"If you are as lucky as I am, it is worthwhile giving money back to worthy causes,"[2] said Gates. Gates's vast personal fortune has the potential to do an enormous amount of good in the world. The example he sets by how he distributes that fortune may have enormous value beyond his own billions. It may inspire other wealthy businessmen and women, now and in the future, to distribute more of their own fortunes to worthy charities worldwide.

Gates is not concerned about how he is perceived personally, but he is concerned about how people view his company. When asked how he thought others viewed him, Gates said, "When people think of me they probably think of some simple thing, like, 'Okay, Windows gave me a funny error message today— couldn't he have done better?' And the answer is 'Yep!' . . . We will do better."[3]

The Bill Gates story is far from over. He has become the wealthiest person in the world as a result of his business dealings in computers and computer software. He has shaped the way the world communicates and uses information. His greatest accomplishments, though, may still lie ahead.

CHRONOLOGY

1955 William Henry Gates III is born in Seattle, Washington, on October 28.

1967 Gates meets Paul Allen, a close friend and, later, a co-founder of Microsoft.

1968 Gates encounters his first computer, at the Lakeside School.

1973 Gates enters Harvard University.

1975 The Micro-soft partnership of Gates and Paul Allen is created.

1980 IBM asks Micro-soft to provide an operating system for their first personal computer.

1983 Microsoft introduces its Microsoft Word word processing program.

1985 The Windows 1.0 operating system is released.

1986 Bill Gates becomes a billionaire at the age of thirty-one; Microsoft becomes a public company on March 13.

1994 Bill Gates and Melinda French marry on January 1.

1995 Gates's first book, *The Road Ahead,* is published.

1996 The Gates's first child, Jennifer Katharine, is born.

1997 The Bill and Melinda Gates Foundation, a charitable organization, is formed.

1998 The U.S. government files an antitrust lawsuit against Microsoft on May 18; the Windows 98 operating system is released; on October 19, the trial begins in the U.S. government's case against Microsoft.

1999 The Gates's son, Rory John, is born; Gates's second book, *Business @ The Speed Of Thought,* is published; on November 5, the court declares Microsoft a monopoly.

2000 Gates resigns as Microsoft CEO; on June 7, the court orders that Microsoft be broken up.

2001 On June 28, a federal appeals court overturns the June 7, 2000, ruling; on September 6, the U.S. Justice Department says it no longer wants to break up Microsoft; Microsoft releases its XP operating system and the Xbox gaming system.

CHAPTER NOTES

CHAPTER ONE. Giving Back

1. "Ted Turner Donates $1 billion To 'U.N. Causes'", *CNN.com,* September 19, 1997, <http://europe.cnn.com/US/9709/18/turner.gift/> (April 2, 2002).

2. "The Top 25," *The Forbes Four Hundred,* 1997 edition, p.152.

3. Jean Strouse, "How To Give Away $21.8 Billion," *The New York Times,* April 16, 2000, p. 56.

4. Laurie Dhue, "Sharing The Wealth," *CNN.com,* September 19, 1997, <http://www1.cnn.com/US/9709/19/donations/> (April 2, 2002).

5. *Recent Foundation Grants,* The Bill & Melinda Gates Foundation, <http://www.gatesfoundation.org/globalhealth/vaccines/announcements/announce-84.htm> (April 2, 2002).

6. *Bill Gates's Comments at World Economic Forum,* Annual Meeting 2001, Davos, Switzerland, <http://www.gatesfoundation.org/mediacenter/speeches/davos_trans.htm> (April 2, 2002).

7. Strouse, p. 56.

CHAPTER TWO. Deep Roots in Seattle

1. David Allison, *Bill Gates Interview,* The National Museum of Natural History, Smithsonian Institution, 1993, <http://americanhistory.si.edu/csr/comphist/gates.htm> (April 2, 2002).

2. "The Gates Operating System", *Time.com,* January 13, 1997, <http://www.time.com/time/gates/gates2.html> (April 2, 2002).

3. Avina Lobo, "Profile: Bill Gates," *ZDNet India,* September 15, 2000, <http://www.zdnetindia.com/news/features/stories/6545.html> (September 1, 2001).

4. Mark Leibovich, "Alter Egos," *The Washington Post,* January 2, 2001, <http://www.washtech.com/news/software/6264-1.html> (April 2, 2002).

5. Lobo.

6. Allison.

7. Ibid.

8   Ibid.

CHAPTER THREE. A Computer in Every Home

1. University of Virginia, Department of Computer Science, <http://www.cs .virginia.edu/brochure/museum/altair.html> (April 2, 2002).

2. David Allison, *Bill Gates Interview,* The National Museum of Natural History, Smithsonian Institution, 1993, <http://americanhistory.si.edu/ csr/comphist/gates.htm> (April 2, 2002).

CHAPTER FOUR. Billionaires and Browser Wars

1. Evan Marcus, *Bill Gates Net Worth Page,* 2001, <http://www.quuxuum.org/ ~evan/bgnw.html> (April 2, 2002).

2. "Great Entrepreneurs," *MyPrimeTime.com,* 1999, <http://www. myprimetime.com/work/ge/gatesbio/index.shtml> (April 2, 2002).

3. Bill Gates, *The Road Ahead* (New York: Viking Penguin, 1995), p. xii.

4. Jennifer Powell, "Lessons from the Browser War (1995-2000)", *Smart Business,* March 2000, <http://www.zdnet.com/smartbusinessmag/ stories/all/0,6605,2429467,00.html> (April 2, 2002).

5. "Microsoft Rivals Say Browser War Is Really about Windows", *CNN.com,* October 20, 1997, <http"//www.cnn.com/TECH/9710/20/ microsoft.impact/> (April 2, 2002).

6. Ibid.

7. *Microsoft, Government to Face Off?* Associated Press, May 18, 1998, <http://www.channel2000.com/news/stories/news-980517-180343 .html>. (September 1, 2001).

CHAPTER FIVE. Trial by Fire

1. *Press Release: Justice Department Files Antitrust Suit Against Microsoft For Unlawfully Monopolizing Computer Software Markets,* Department of Justice, May 18, 1998, <http://www.usdoj.gov/atr/public/press_releases/ 1998/1764.htm> (April 2, 2002).

2. "Microsoft Response to Filing of Antitrust Suits", *Tech Law Journal.com,* May 18, 1998, <http://www.techlawjournal.com/courts/dojvmsft2/80518msft.htm> (April 2, 2002).

3. James Grimaldi, "U.S. Targets Bill Gates in First Day of Microsoft Trial," *Seattle Times,* October 19, 1998, p.1.

4. "The Missing Evidence in the Microsoft Case," *USA Today.com,* August 9, 1999, <http://www.usatoday.com/news/comment/columnists/freeman/ncjf13.htm> (April 2, 2002).

5. James Grimaldi, "Judge Rules Microsoft a Monopoly," *Seattle Times,* November 6, 1999, p. 1.

6. "In Their Own Words," *Seattle Times.com,* November 6, 1999, <http://seattletimes.nwsource.com/news/technology/html98/reax_19991106.html> (April 2, 2002).

CHAPTER SIX. Epilogue

1. Ann Knowles, "Gates 'Bets The Company' On Microsoft.Net Strategy", *eWeek,* June 22, 2000, <http://www.zdnet.com/eweek/stories/general/0,11011,2592662,00.html> (September 1, 2001).

2. David F. Salisbury, "Gates: Software Changing The 'Very Mechanism of Capitalism,'" *Stanford Online Report,* January 28, 1998, <http://www.stanford.edu/dept/news/report/news/january28/gates128.html> (April 2, 2002).

3. "Bill Gates Q&A," *USAToday.com,* September 9, 1998, <http://www.usatoday.com/life/cyber/tech/cti483htm> (September 1, 2001).

GLOSSARY

BASIC—A simple computer language that was in widespread use in the early 1970s. BASIC stands for Beginners All-purpose Symbolic Instruction Code.

browser—The software that enables a computer to retrieve and display documents posted to the World Wide Web.

bug—An error in a computer program.

bytes—The building blocks of computer information, expressed as ones and zeroes; one byte is composed of eight bits (a single zero or one).

CEO—Chief Executive Officer, the person in a company who is responsible for the overall activities of that company.

code—A series of instructions to a computer, written in a language that the computer can understand. Most often, code refers to the fundamental instructions that tell a computer how it should operate.

computer chip—The "brain" of a computer, the core inside which information processing takes place.

e-mail—Electronic mail, a way of sending messages from one computer user to another.

hard drive—The storage area inside a computer where programs and documents are kept.

Internet—The system of worldwide connected computer networks, of which the World Wide Web is a part.

litigation—The process of contesting something in law through the courts.

monopoly—Exclusive possession and control of a product or service.

operating system—The software that allows a computer to operate.

PC—A personal computer.

philanthropy—The practice of donating money to promote human welfare. The term is usually used to refer to large donations by very wealthy individuals or companies.

software—Computer programs (as opposed to "hardware" which are the machines themselves).

stock market—A financial exchange where investments in a company are bought, sold, and traded. Examples of stock markets include the New York Stock Exchange and the American Stock Exchange.

terminal—A device usually consisting of a keyboard and a teletype printer, used for entering information into a computer.

World Wide Web—The World Wide Web consists of millions of Web pages, which can link to one another in order to make information easier to find.

FURTHER READING

Connolly, Sean. *Bill Gates.* Crystal Lake, Illinois: Heinemann Library, 1998.

Dearlove, Des. *Business the Bill Gates Way.* Tulsa, Oklahoma: Capstone Publishing, 2001.

Gates, Bill. *Business @ The Speed Of Thought: Using A Digital Nervous System.* New York: Warner Books, 1999.

_____. *The Road Ahead.* New York: Viking Penguin, 1995.

Heller, Robert. *Bill Gates.* New York: Dorling Kindersley Publishing, Inc., 2000.

Lesinski, Jeanne M. *Bill Gates.* Minneapolis, Minnesota: Lerner Publications Company, 2000.

Manes, Stephen and Andrews, Paul. *Gates: How Microsoft's Mogul Reinvented an Industry—and Made Himself the Richest Man in America.* New York: Touchstone Books, 1994.

Wood, Sara. *Bill Gates: Computer Giant.* New York: Raintree Steck-Vaughn Publishers, 2002.

Woog, Adam. *Bill Gates.* Farmington Hills, Michigan: Gale Group, 1998.

Wukovits, John. *Bill Gates: Software King.* London: Franklin Watts, 2000.

INTERNET ADDRESSES

Bill Gates' home page, published on the Microsoft Web site.
http://www.microsoft.com/billgates/default.asp

The home page of the Bill and Melinda Gates Foundation.
http://www.gatesfoundation.org

Transcript of a 1993 "Video History Interview" with Bill Gates, conducted by David Allison on behalf of the Smithsonian Institution's National Museum of American History.
http://americanhistory.si.edu/csr/comphist/gates.htm

INDEX